Pennine Motor Services, Skipton

1925 to 2014

by Stuart Emmett

RHE 31W approaches Burnley on Colne Road. OS

Stenlake Publishing Ltd

Text © Stuart Emmett, 2024.
First published in the United Kingdom, 2024, reprinted 2025,
by Stenlake Publishing Ltd,
54-58 Mill Square,
Catrine, Ayrshire,
KA5 6RD

Telephone: 01290 551122
www.stenlake.co.uk

ISBN 9781840339635

**The publishers regret that they cannot supply
copies of any pictures featured in this book.**

The proceeds from the book sales, after deduction of costs, are going 100% to assist on bus preservation/archives. The author and some of the image providers have supplied their services free of charge.

Acknowledgements

Unless stated below, the pictures are from my own collection of family pictures and other sources, some of which have proved impossible to accredit, for which I apologise.

Pictures/images are from in no specific order: Keith Newton, Don McKeown, Colin Robinson, Bob Downham, Peter Gaunt, Phil Howard, Tony Greaves and from the following image providers: P.M. Photography, Wikki Commons, The Omnibus Society, Ribble Enthusiasts Club.

NWT 839V from 1980 and the last new Plaxton bus purchased. A Leyland Leopard with Plaxton Supreme Express body it was registered JIL 4698 in 1994 and was withdrawn in 1997 to be replaced by a Leyland National LN11 that received this JIL registration.

The Company's Development/Time Line

Skipton is a small market town known as the "Gateway to the Dales" and is a central transport location being at the junction of the A65 and A59 roads. The A65 goes from Leeds, Ilkey and Otley up to Kendal in the Lake District (and 4 miles from Skipton passes Gargrave, the traditional HQ of Pennine). The A59 heads from York, Harrogate, Clitheroe, Preston, and Liverpool. Into this mix is the A629 to Skipton from Keighley and Bradford along with the B6265 from Grassington and the Dales.

Skipton therefore tends always to be a busy place and this has resulted in some long-distance bus routes. Additionally, the town attracts visitors from the small towns and villages in Ribblesdale, Airedale and Wharfedale, including the conurbations of Burnley/Colne and Leeds/Bradford, some 20 to 25 miles away.

1925: Pennine Motor Services was started at the end of 1925 by brothers Arthur and Vic Simpson, from a family of stonemasons, who owned and ran a garage at Albion Place, Skipton selling cars and motorcycles, and their brother-in-law Jim Windle, a bus driver who had the idea of running buses due to his employment with Castle Motors, Skipton. The name Pennine was chosen as being appropriate to their operating area. The first service, to Settle, ran from Skipton and started outside Dobson's Chemist, in Skipton High Street. Jim Windle parked the first bus outside Dobson's as he knew the owner. Timings were coordinated with Hull's 1921 service from Skipton to Gargrave.

1926: Pennine bought Richard and John Lamb of Settle for their Settle to Ingleton route, whilst Lamb kept their route to Horton in Ribblesdale. This route later passed to Alderson, then to Hillcrest Coaches/E. Lamb in August 1962 and to Whaites, Settle from March 1974, to Ingfield/Northern Rose in 1994 and was later operated by North Yorkshire CC.

Rather ominously, County Motors of Lancaster started running from Morecambe into Skipton via Ingleton and Settle with three trips a day extended into Skipton. However, they cooperated with Pennine on the timings between Skipton and Ingleton.

1927: Pennine bought the Gargrave service of Arthur Hull of Skipton and ran around twenty buses a day to Gargrave.

1928: Ribble bought a controlling share of County of Lancaster in July after getting authorisation for a service to Ingleton and Skipton that March. In September, maybe as retaliation, Pennine started running into Lancaster and Morecambe with four daily through services and approx. every hour to Settle.

A summer Sunday one round trip route to Windermere was also run and this was to be the longest Pennine stage bus route.

Premises were bought at Gargrave near the Grouse Hotel and were retained until 2006.

Morecambe with maroon liveried WW 9818 that was one of two Leyland TS2 Tigers bought in 1929 with Leyland bus bodies. It lasted until 1949.

Gargrave depot and yard in the late 1990s. Phil Howard

The "back lot" at Gargrave in the 1980s with an HWU and friend.

1929 Leyland TS2 WW 9817 in the former maroon livery at Windermere. WW 9817 was rebodied by Burlingham C32F in 1938 and lasted until 1953. The Burlingham coach body was then fitted to 1936 AWX 764 which ran until 1958, latterly in the orange and cream coach livery.

1929: In January Ribble bought out County of Lancaster. Pennine had further competition, on the route to Ingleton, from Castle Motors of Skipton, who were also now owned by Ribble who had bought them for their routes to Colne and Earby. So, intense competition then took place with Ribble.

1930: Although competition continued, it soon seemed Pennine would not be shaken off as Skipton passengers preferred to use their buses. Ribble therefore chose to have discussions with Pennine. An agreement was made whereby Pennine gave up their 1928-started summer Sunday Windermere service and more importantly, a 50/50 sharing was to begin in 1931. Ribble also agreed to undertake the administration in return for a space at Pennine's Ingleton depot on a nominal rent.

The former maroon livery with gold lining changed, Lion WX 2979 being delivered in orange with a black roof and a duck egg blue (grey) stripe. This livery is thought to have been inspired by the shirts of the Leyland Motors football team.

All-Leyland Lion LT1 WX 2979 in the then new livery in 1930. It was rebodied in 1944 with a Burlingham UB32F body and ran on until 1951. OS

1931: A formal agreement with Pennine and Ribble was launched on 1st January. This was to share the mileage and fares on a 50/50 basis; Ribble did the administration and a weekly cheque was sent to Pennine.

Pennine ran mainly to Ingleton, and Ribble ran from there to Lancaster and Morecambe. Pennine had earlier-run four times daily through buses to Morecambe. From May they used the Damside Street Bus Station in Lancaster. Later in the year, the Skipton to Morecambe route appears to have been reduced to just one Pennine morning return journey from Ingleton to Morecambe and return to Skipton. As for Ribble, their only journeys east of Ingleton to Skipton were two round trips on a Sunday (in 1977 for example, the 0948 ex Lancaster and return at 1235 and the 1548 returning from Skipton at 1835 hours).

AEC Regal 662 WX 7431 leaves Skipton. It was new in 1931 and would be rebodied in 1948 by Burlingham. This bus from new had orange, black and duck egg blue livery, although the specific film and processing used does not clearly differentiate between the orange and black.

1933: Pennine started a route to Malham from Skipton.

1935: Pennine bought, with Ribble MS, Parker, Airton t/a Malhamdale Motors who had a service to Malham that ran three times a day with six trips on Saturday.

1936: The Malham route had become 50/50 with Ribble, as had the Morecambe route in 1931. Ribble used route numbers for the Morecambe route from 1936, with a different series for the Lancashire and Yorkshire departure towns, for example:

> 37 to 44 Lancaster to Ingleton, via either Wennington, Millhouses, and Burton in Lonsdale or just via Millhouses, with the 38, 40, 42 and 44, extended to Skipton and the 41/42 starting in Morecambe. From Skipton examples are the 220 to Hellifield, 230 to Settle, 240 to Austwick, 250/260 to Ingleton.

Later times with a Ribble 1964 Leyland Leopard/Marshall heading on 42 short to Ingleton. REC

AWX 764 with AWX 763 were 1936 Leyland Tigers TS7 with Leyland B32F bodies. 764 was to be rebodied in 1953 with the Burlingham coach body from WW 9817 and then stayed with Pennine until 1958. 763 left in 1954 and the chassis went to Malta and became FBY 716. OS

Malta FBY 716 with local body on former Pennine AWX 763. Creative Commons Attribution-Share Alike 2.0 Generic licence.

1939 to 1945: The workforce was halved from 34 to 17 due to military "call ups" and conductresses were brought in, with ten being employed by 1941. With parts and maintenance people in short supply, the fleet suffered and from 1945 some buses were rebodied, and second-hand buses were also delivered.

1946 to 1949: Two new Leyland PS were delivered in 1947 (with Burlingham bus bodies) and two more in 1949 (coaches from Wilkes & Mead and from Burlingham). These were complemented by two AEC Regals from Halifax CT in 1949 with Roe and Park Royal bodies and had been new in 1935 and 1939 respectively. Additionally, 1931 Regal WX 7431 was also rebodied by Burlingham.

1935 JX 3424 AEC Regal/Roe came from Halifax in 1949, stayed until 1955 and helped with the post-war boom in traffic.

1938 JX 6560 AEC Regal/PRV was another former Halifax bus bought in 1949 and left in 1952. It is at Gargrave inbound for Skipton with one of the AWXs. OS

At Gargrave, WX 7431, the 1931 AEC Regal, now with a 1948 Burlingham B35F body and an AEC diesel engine. It worked until 1957.

1950: Waller Hill Bus Station in Skipton was opened on 8th May and replaced the former street stands.

1951: Pennine bought their first underfloor engined bus (MTC 757) in November, the same month as a 1936 bus (ATE 804) entered service from Lancashire United. Quite a contrast in the two technologies!

More second-hand buses to assist in increased traffic with Leyland TS7 ATE 804 bought in November 1951 preceded in October 1951 by sister ATE 801. Both were withdrawn in October 1956.

1956: A small depot opened in Skipton. This was on Jerry Croft off the High Street alongside the town hall that accessed a large car park. The depot closed in 2003 (and another view of the depot follows later in this book).

Jerry Croft, Skipton with RWY379M. The small depot is the "dark hole" at the back. PM

Inside the Skipton depot. Tony Greaves

1960: Tiger JWT 724 was fitted with ram air doors and nearside slanted front window for OMO on the Malham route.

1963: Pennine opened their new build two-bus garage at Settle that used stone from the demolished Grammar School in Giggleswick.

2002 Dart D8 came to Pennine in 2012 and was there to the end in 2014. It is seen here loading alongside the small Settle depot. Don McKeown

Route Development 1925 to 1960s.

Note: these tables are indicative times from the respective dates.

From	To (and miles from Skipton)	Via	From	Headway	JT
+Skipton	**Settle**, Market Square (16 miles)	Gargrave Hellifield, Long Preston	24th Dec 1925 with five trips Monday to Saturday.	1930s hourly.	60 minutes
			1961/62	Fourteen trips Monday to Friday and nine on Tuesday with sixteen trips on Saturday and twelve trips on Sunday	53 mins
	Ingleton, Ingleton Hotel, later to Three Horse Shoes. (26 miles)	As above to Settle, then Giggleswick, Clapham.	1926	1930s every 90 minutes with nine journeys a day, ten on Saturday and eight on Sunday.	2 hours
			1961/62	Nine trips Monday/Wednesday to Friday and ten on Tuesday with twelve trips on Saturday and eight trips on Sunday.	1 hour 23 minutes

+ Joint with Ribble

From	To (and miles from Skipton)	Via	From	Headway	JT
	Lancaster, Dalton Square, then to Damside Street, this was later developed as the Cable Street Bus Station. (42 miles)	As above to Ingleton, then three variations. (1) Burton in Lonsdale, High and Lower Bentham, Mill Houses, Wray, Hornby, Caton. (2) Burton in Lonsdale, High and Lower Bentham, Wennington, Wray, Hornby, Caton. (3) Burton in Lonsdale, Cantsfield, Melling, Hornby, Caton.	1928	1930s every 3 hours. Four journeys a Monday to Friday.	3 hours
	Morecambe, Euston Road Bus Station. (46 miles)	As above to Lancaster, then via Torrisholme.	1928 1961/62	Initially four a day but reduced back in 1931. One direct trip Monday to Friday.	3 hours 20 minutes 3 hours

From	To (and miles from Skipton)	Via	From	Headway	JT
Skipton	**Windermere** (57 miles)	As above to Ingleton, then via Kendal.	Started 1928. Finished on 21-09-1930.	One trip on Summer Sunday.	Dropped as part of the 1930 agreement with Ribble.
+Skipton	**Malham**, Buck Hotel. (11 miles)	Gargrave, Airton.	1933 1961/62	Eight trips, ten on Saturday. Five trips Monday, Wendesday, Friday, and four trips Tuesday and Thursday, with six Saturday and two Sunday.	43 minutes 41 minutes
Settle	**Tosside**, Temperance Hotel. (8.5 miles)	Rathmell, Wigglesworth.	1928, 1931 and around 1945 are reported. 1961/62	One trip with short on Tuesday. Two trips on Tuesday only and connected with the 1034 from Skipton and the 1244 from Lancaster.	35 minutes

+ Joint with Ribble

1930s: Excursions and tours from Skipton, Airton, Hellifield, Barnoldswick and added later, Settle, Barnoldswick, Embsay.

Works Service from Barnoldswick (Park Road) to Gargrave J&J factory.

Records show that both Ribble and Pennine used four buses each as follows:

- Ribble with two from Ingleton, one from Lancaster and one (on Sunday only) from Skipton.
- Pennine providing one from Ingleton, two from Settle and one from Skipton.

Pennine was also said to have been a pool member on the Leeds to Morecambe express route, with the miles due, being instead used on stage routes (with the cooperation of Ribble). However, this service is only shown in timetables as an X88 West Yorkshire route and was not even shown as being joint with Ribble. Certainly, Pennine did operate on this route on hire to West Yorkshire, as indeed did many other operators, especially in the peak summer months.

The excursions and tours were in summer 1961, jointly marketed, as shown in this leaflet. Departures were at varied times dependent on the destination, for example.

- Before 1000 to Chester, various Lake District destinations, Blackpool, Bridlington, Whitby

- 1000 to 1400 to Richmond, Catterick, York, Sedbergh, Ripon, Harrogate

- 1800 to Buckden, Wigglesworth, Slaidburn, Bronte country

All had the same "due back" time of 2130 hours.

In summer 1959 the joint marketing excluded West Yorkshire RCC.

Timeline continued

1967: Following the conversion of the Malham route in 1960, OMO was now progressively started on all of the other routes. The Simpson/Windle partnership included six families as sons/son-in-laws had entered the business. However, the Windles sold out to the remaining partners and Arthur Simpson drew a new agreement with those partners that remained.

1969: Tilling's West Yorkshire and BET's Ribble became part of the National Bus Company (NBC) and major changes were to come for Skipton-based routes. These changes meant Pennine gained routes.

1970: By now Pennine was a 100% OMO and staffing had been reduced from thirty-three to twenty-three.

1971: the last new "pure" stage buses arrived with HWU 816/7J Leyland Leopards with BET style Willowbrook DP49F bodies. They had been preceeded in 1969/1970 by similar CWT 474H and CWU 101H.

CWT 474H was new in 1969. Keith Newton

1972: Pennine took over Ezra Laycock of Barnoldswick with their routes from Skipton to Carleton and Barnoldswick (later numbered 212 and 211), with the Laycock school contracts given away. Laycock kept part of the Barnoldswick premises and Pennine used the other part for the overnighting of two buses. The final day for Laycock was 11th August 1972. A large crowd gathered for the last and newest bus, Leyland Leopard number 93.

The fleet Pennine took over was as follows:

- 74 BCK 437 came from Ribble in July 1966 and was a Leyland PD1A with Burlingham body.
- 80 ECK 927 came from Ribble in August 1968 and was an all-Leyland double decker.
- 83 968 CWL was an AEC Regent V from City of Oxford Motor Services with Weymann body and came in February 1970.
- 84 to 86 and 89, 94/95 (OWX 144, XHW408/409/401, RWW 977/985), were Bristol LS5Gs with ECW bodies new to West Yorkshire RCC and Bristol OC and bought in 1970/1971.
- 90 to 92 MYG 759 to 761K were new in January 1972 and were Bedford YRQs with Plaxton Express bodies.
- 93 OWY 197K was new in April 1972 and was a Leyland PSU3B/4R with Plaxton Express body.

As Pennine was not interested in the Laycock works and school contracts, all the double deckers used on such work went. One of the Bristol LSs did run for a week or so on the Carleton route, before being sold on, like all the others. Only Plaxtons 90 to 93 were to enter full service with Pennine on the stage routes.

Some of the Laycock buses not required by Pennine.

Laycock 89, XHW 401 was one of the buses soon sold off by Pennine. Keith Newton

1974: The April local government reorganisation meant Skipton left the West Riding of Yorkshire and became part of North Yorkshire. Bus operations in West Yorkshire were grouped into the West Yorkshire PTE (WYPTE). Also, Ribble, following National Bus directives, were soon to close its Skipton operations.

Pennine were active in hiring coaches to other operators and here on Saturday 27th July 1974 is RWY 378M on hire to National Travel West loading at Blackpool Corporation Depot Yard, whilst duplicating the 0850hours route 981, to Edinburgh. Pennine standardised from 1973 to 1990 on Plaxton coaches, especially the Express versions. RWY 378M was new in April 1974. It had a short life as it suffered a fatal fire in October 1980. R. Downham

1976: Ribble closed their Skipton depot on 23rd May 1976 and their Broughton Road depot was sold to Pennine MS. This depot had come to Ribble from the Old Bill Motors Bus Service that Ribble had taken over in 1928; however, Pennine rented the depot out to a car exhaust/tyre company who left in 2003. Pennine finally moved in March 2006, when it then became the main depot.

Ribble Skipton depot ran on the following routes:

- 210 Skipton – Malham (joint with Pennine).
- 230 Skipton – Eastby via Embsay (the former S6 until March 1970).
- 233 Skipton – Bolton Abbey via Embsay and Halton East (the former S3 until March 1970).
- 235 Skipton bus station – Broughton Road bus depot (effectively a positioning service).
- 281 Skipton – Colne.
- 580/581/582 Skipton – Lancaster – Morecambe (joint with Pennine).
- X43 Skipton – Manchester.

Ribble now operated these routes from the WY Skipton depot. However, the local Ribble 230 and 233 routes to Eastby via Embsay and to Bolton Abbey via Embsay and Halton East, passed over to West Yorkshire from 23rd May 1976 and were re-numbered 75 and 76.

Skipton Bus Station with a West Yorkshire RE (their SRG class), Pennine NWT 807 laying over and Ribble 673 on the 230 (former S6) to Embsay. Ten Ribble buses in this CRN/DRNxxxD batch were sold to the Isle of Man in late 1979/early 1980 where they operated up to October 1982 and May 1985.

1977: Ribble stopped using the West Yorkshire depot in January 1977 and their remaining Skipton routes were transferred to the Ribble Clitheroe and Burnley depots. After objection from Wallace Arnold over a Pennine excursion and tours licence, this was refused. However, the Pennine application for tours to Holland were not objected to, so Pennine ran there for some years.

Seen in Blackpool Coach Park on 24th June 1978 is UWR 712R at Blackpool Coach Park. The first Plaxton Supreme Express delivered in 1977 was followed by two others in 1978 and 1980.
R. Downham

1980: The last new Leyland/Plaxton NWT 839V arrived. Thereafter from 1981, the purchases of Leyland/Plaxtons were second-hand. The last new buses were two 1991 Leyland Swifts that were quickly sold after nine months.

1983: West Yorkshire closed its Skipton depot on 25th June 1983 (planned originally for the 13th August 1983) and their routes were now operated from their Grassington and Keighley depots. The closure was said to be due to lack of subsidies from NYCC.

1986/1987: Bus de-regulation brought in a challenging and changing period with many upheavals to the former ways of operating. Whilst some operators anticipated the changes and prepared themselves as best they could, others took a more pragmatic view and choose to wait and see what happened. It was also a challenging time for bus enthusiasts who tried to "keep up"!

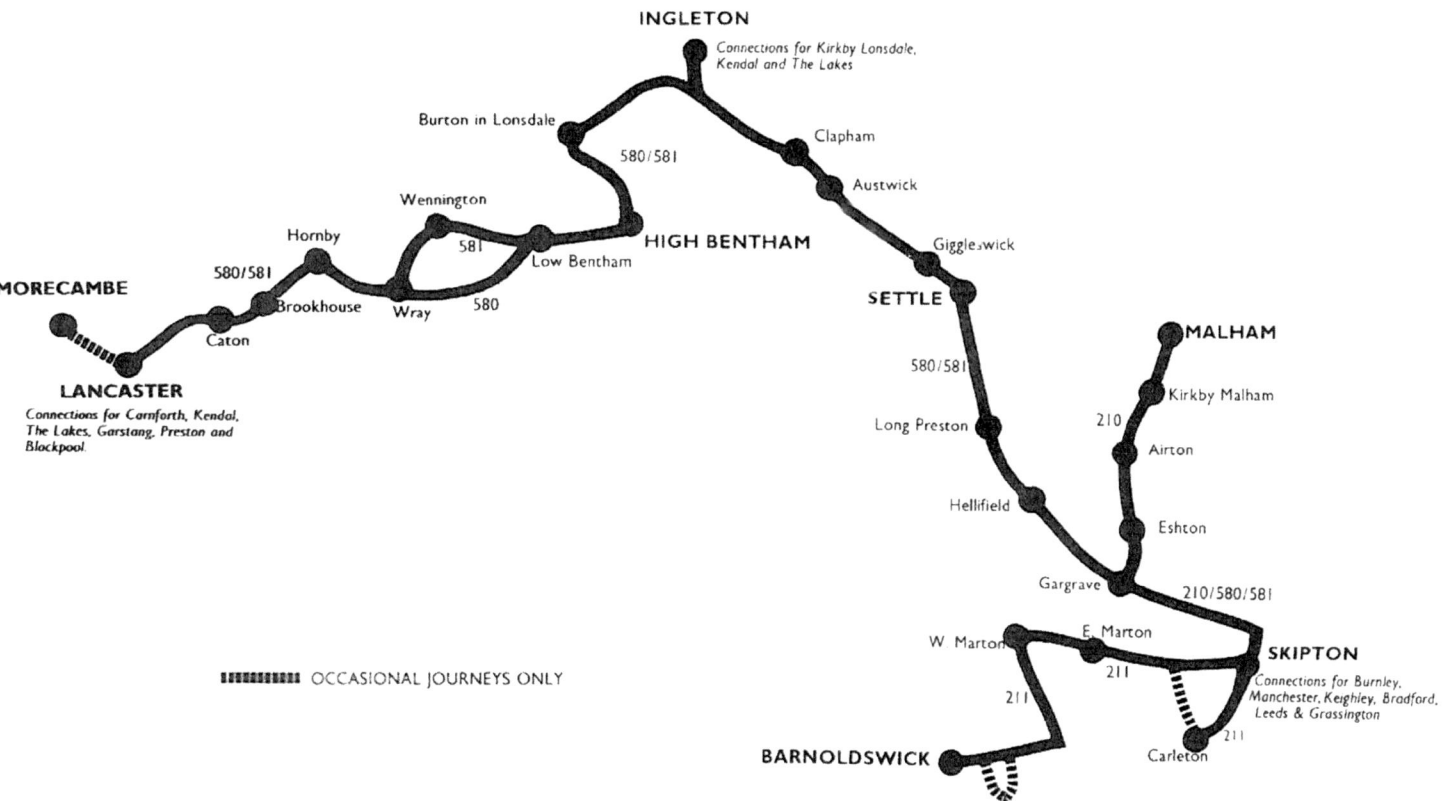

In May 1986 the above map (in leaflet 82 of Ribble), gives a view of the bus services; all was soon to change from a long-term stable relationship.

Bus de-regulation came in on 26th October following the 1985 Transport Act. Noncommercial routes went out to tender and joint operations were not allowed. The situation also became "complicated" for Pennine, as they preferred to operate commercially.

West Yorkshire did not tender for the local Skipton Horse Close/Shortbank routes 73/74. However, Pennine gained them and numbered them as route 216. Pennine also gained the WY 75 route from Skipton to Embsay/Eastby and numbered it route 214. The 76 Bolton Abbey route was retained by West Yorkshire and extended to Grassington, with two school bus journeys daily, and one public journey on Mon/Wed/Friday. The 76 also linked at Grassington, to the direct West Yorkshire Skipton to Grassington service and the West Yorkshire route 772, from Ilkey to Bolton Abbey and Grassington, was then cut back to just one Monday to Friday journey.

West Yorkshire short Leyland National 1009 approaching Bolton Abbey on the Grassington extension.
Keith Newton

The Pennine Morecambe route with effectively, the Ribble leg, from Ingleton and the Pennine leg, from Ingleton to Skipton, were each put out for tender by the relative County Councils. Ribble won their leg for weekdays and Lancaster City Transport got Sundays. Pennine continued for a brief time duplicating the tendered route to Ingleton but in 1987 they cut back to Giggleswick, just a few minutes past Settle. This meant the end of the Ingleton depot, shared with Ribble, which had space for four buses. Meanwhile, the Settle to Ingleton section was tendered as a NYCC subsidised route and run by Ribble and then by Lancaster CT and later, by a local Settle operator. Finally, in 2014, Kirkby Lonsdale Coaches successfully stepped in on this route.

Ribble also stopped the X43 to Manchester at Nelson and Pennine started a service numbered 211 to link from Skipton. Eventually, however, Lancashire County Council were required to tender, and Burnley & Pendle won the whole route from Skipton to Burnley. They soon found the Colne to Skipton leg not profitable and withdrew on 10th April 1988 – the die was then cast for later complications to arise on this route. Meanwhile, Pennine decided to run competitively to Burnley with route 215.

The 215 Burnley route started on the 15th March and then the 211 to Nelson was withdrawn.

An unusual "alleged" purchase by Pennine was BKC 288K, an Atlantean/Alexander H74F from Merseyside PTE. Records with Pennine, however, show it was purchased in September 1987 and was out of service by August 1989. Its purpose is unknown, and it was possibly used, still in Merseyside livery, on a works contract. However, doubt remains as the bus was photographed in January 1988 working with Four Seasons in Leeds.

"Ghost" bus BKC 288K.

Route Development 1970s to 1990s.

From & Route Number	To	Via	From	Headway Mon-Fri	JT
Skipton 585/586	Settle via Tosside.	Gargrave Hellifield, Long Preston, Wigglesworth, Tosside, Wigglesworth, Rathmell.	May 1978 when into the Skipton to Settle service.	Tuesday one trip diversion from the "main" 580 route.	Unknown
				Gone by 1986 and later run by NYCC Horton in Ribblesdale-Settle-Tosside.	Unknown

From & Route Number	To	Via	From	Headway Mon-Fri	JT
Skipton 580	Morecambe	Gargrave Hellifield, Long Preston, Settle, Giggleswick Clapham, Ingleton, Burton, Hi and Lower Bentham, Millhouses, Wray, Hornby, Caton, Lancaster.	Up to October 1986.	Three to Settle. Two to G/Wick. Six to Ingleton. Four to Lancaster. One a day from Ingleton to Morecambe that returns to Skipton.	48 mins 50 mins 74 mins 2 hrs 27 mins 2 hrs 40 mins
Skipton 581	Lancaster	Via Wennington instead of Millhouses.	Up to October 1986.	Two of the above Lancaster trips.	
Skipton 580	Ingleton	As bove.	October 1986 to 1987.	Four a day duplicating the NYCC operator** from Settle to Ingleton.	
Skipton 580	Giggleswick	Gargrave Hellifield, Long Preston, Settle.	From March 1987 to the end.	Thirteen a day to Giggleswick.	45 mins
Skipton 210	Malham (Buck Hotel)	Gargrave, Eshton, Airton, Kirkby Malham.	1933. Fom May 1986 to the end.	Three a day, four on Wednesday. Two a day (plus one journey a day via J&J Gargrave).	45 mins 40 mins

From & Route Number	To	Via	From	Headway Mon-Fri	JT
Skipton 211	B/Wick	Carleton, West & East Marton. ***	August 1972 ex Laycock. From 15th March 1987 was joined to Burnley route (see rt.215), and then ran via Thornton & Earby.	Twelve a day (five trips from Skipton via Coates Est. Barnoldswick).	25 mins
Skipton 211	B/Wick	Earby	June 1987	One a day at 0655 ex Barnoldswick and 1620 ex Skipton.	
Skipton 212*	Carleton (Was served by route 211 from 1972).		15th March 1987	Thirteen a day	10 mins
Skipton 214* (Ex Ribble S6/230 and WY 75).	Eastby Cut back to Embsay in 1994.	Embsay	27th October 1986 ex WY	Thirteen a day to Embsay including five a day to Eastby.	15 mins 10 mins
Skipton 215	Nelson	Thornton, Earby, Kilbrook, Foulridge, Colne.	27th October 1986 to 14th March 1987.	Thirteen a day and intended to connect jwith Ribble X43 at Nelson.	45 mins
	Burnley	Thornton, Earby, Kelbrook, B'wick, Kelbrook, Colne, Nelson.	From 15th March 1987.	Hourly	70/75 mins

From & Route Number	To	Via	From	Headway Mon-Fri	JT
Skipton 216*	Horse Close and Greatwood Estates Circular.	Skipton local.	May 1992 from K&D	Thirteen a day.	20 mins round trip.
Barnoldswick 218 Works service.	Johnson & Johnson Gargrave.	Thornton, Coates Estate, Barnoldswick, Kelbrook, Earby, Thornton.	By 1999	One round trip a day.	55 mins

*   Some timings were operationally interlinked, especially with the Burnley route at Skipton. From Skipton the local routes of Skipton-Embsay-Skipton-Carleton-Skipton-Horse Close-Skipton took around 52mins.

** Ingleton to Settle was won by Ribble from October 1986 to 3rd April 1988, then from 5th April 1988 by the former Lancaster CT, their route 81 Lancaster, Hornby, Kirkby Lonsdale, Ingleton to Settle with one journey Mon to Sat only. Both operators connected with Pennine at Settle.

*** West and East Marton continued to be served from Skipton by the former Ribble X27 route to Clitheroe, Preston, Southport, and Liverpool that from 1986 was run as far as Preston by various operators, such as Preston CT, Transdev Lancashire United and Stagecoach.

1988: West Yorkshire RCC was sold by a management buyout (the AJS Group) and three companies were eventually formed, Keighley and District, Harrogate and District, and Yorkshire Coastliner, based in Malton.

K&D ran the former Ribble/WY route 76 Skipton – Embsay – Bolton Abbey – Burnsall – Grassington service. They then were to become part of Transdev, who already owned the former Burnley, Colne and Nelson company now called Transdev Burnley & Pendle.

1991/2: In June 1991, Skipton Busways from Settle, using two old Leyland Nationals, started competing with Pennine and K&D. This was with a Keighley to Settle service numbered 590, and they also competed directly with Pennine on the Skipton local route with a third Leyland National. The Skipton to Settle leg was soon stopped, but their remaining Skipton to Keighley service was increased, so in July 1991, K&D increased their Keighley to Skipton route to three buses per hour.

Other short-term competitors in June 1991 were Pinnacle on the Skipton local routes and also Craven Coachways on the Embsay route. Both, however, left in February 1992 and were soon followed by Skipton Busways in May 1992 when Skipton Busways "de-registered" their remaining services (Skipton local and Keighley). Their three Leyland Nationals went to Sovereign (a Blazefield company who now were the owners of K&D). Effectively it seemed that K&D bought Skipton Busways, with Pennine contributing.

H313 WUA Leyland Swift/Reeves Burgess new in 1991 went in January 1992. Sister H314 WUA had the normal Pennine livery.

1994: The Keighley & District Skipton to Bolton Abbey service went to tender and was won by Pennine, but then confusions happened with the North Yorkshire County Council (NYCC). This led to Pennine's withdrawal from the Bolton Abbey and Eastby routes, apart from morning and afternoon school runs. Later, the Malham route gained a subsidised postbus with lower fares than Pennine. This left once again, only the Pennine school buses running.

1999: Thirteen Leyland Nationals were now in the fleet, and the first second-hand Leyland National came in 1994.

LN10 was formerly JNA 589N and new to Greater Manchester PTE in 1975. It came via another operator to Pennine in 1995. It was re-registered as JIL 7416 in 1996 and was withdrawn in 2001 and replaced by another National. It is seen heading out to Carleton from Skipton. Keith Newton

In the 2000s the industry was changing again with the gradual reduction of subsidies to operators and in the rebate paid for concessionary travel.

2003: The two-bus depot in Jerry Croft, Skipton was closed and the land sold. Pennine were now replacing the Leyland Nationals with second-hand Dennis Darts and had six at the end of 2003.

JIL 7416(LN10) in Jerry Croft, Skipton depot and competing for space with the market trader and dog. Tony Greaves

2006: Pennine moved on 31st March to the former Skipton Ribble Depot they had owned since 1976, and this along with the sale of the Gargrave premises, meant Skipton was now the main Pennine depot.

Outside the second and last Skipton depot on Broughton Road is HWR 449T. This was converted from a former Fishwick of Preston 1979 Leyland Leopard/Plaxton coach registered OCK 452T. The coach came in 1989 and in 1994 was re-registered JIL 4653. On withdrawal in 1995, it became HWR 449T.

2008: Skipton Bus Station was rebuilt in September/October with eight "nose in" stands.

2009: The last two Leyland Nationals were withdrawn.

2010: The fleet of Darts was now nineteen.

2011: Norman Simpson died aged 70 in June and his son Maurice now became the senior partner.

2012: Transdev/Burnley & Pendle started competing on the Burnley route every 30 minutes, with alternative buses running via Barnoldswick or Earby. Pennine's hourly route did a double run from Barnoldswick to Kelbrook to Earby, then back to Kelbrook for Burnley. This meant the B&P service, end to end, was faster. Pennine retaliated with shorts between Barnoldswick to Burnley, but this resulted in further financial losses.

2014: The reduction of subsidies and rebates had a "slow death" cumulative effect for Pennine and on Friday 16th May at 2115 hours, the final bus from Skipton to Settle ran, (Dart D8, KU52 RYG, new in 2002 and bought from Arriva in 2012). Company boss Maurice Simpson blamed a 20% reduction in annual free travel payments from NYCC that cost Pennine £45,000 as well as competition from Transdev on the route to Burnley. He said *"North Yorkshire reimburses 28.4 per cent of free travel whereas Lancashire pays back 56 per cent. That is our problem. There are also too many buses on our main bus route between Skipton and Barnoldswick. We have tried our best to keep going but the situation has got worse over the past four years or so, and we just couldn't carry on. It's a very sad day."*

The company's official announcement said: *"It is with regret that as from the close of business on the 16th May 2014, Pennine Motors will no longer trade as a bus company. I am sure you will appreciate that this has been a very difficult decision for myself and my family as my grandfather founded the business in 1925 together with his brother and brother-in-law, but unfortunately it is no longer financially viable. I would like to thank all our loyal customers for their unwavering support over the last 88 years."*

County, district, and town councillor Robert Heseltine said: *"The orange Pennine buses have been an integral part of the social and commercial fabric of Skipton, wider Craven and East Lancashire for generations. Their loss and the loss of local employment is a great sadness. The Simpson family have a long tradition of bringing economic benefit to Craven. It was they who, in the early 1900s, laid the setts on Skipton High Street. It was Norman Simpson who built the store at the entrance to Jerry Croft which brought Marks & Spencer to Skipton. Hopefully as one door closes another will open for the Simpson family and their employees, but it really is the end of a loved and respected bus transport era."*

The *Craven and Valley Life Magazine* reported *"On Friday 16 May at 9.15pm, the final bus left Stand 3 at Skipton bus station to make the last journey to Settle, and there were lumps in the throats of the locals who turned out to ride the bus one last time or see it rumble down the road"*.

Pennine had covered millions of miles on Yorkshire Dales roads, but now the orange and black buses of Pennine Motor Services had gone and the depots at Skipton, Settle and Barnoldswick were to be sold by auction.

Plaxton Dart D8 (second issue) leaves Skipton as the last bus in service. New in 2002 to Peters of West Bromwich it had come from Arriva. Don McKeown

Final Routes in May 2014

No.	Skipton to	Daily Trips Mon to Fri	Depot
210	Malham	Two	Skipton
212	Carleton	Eleven	Skipton
214	Embsay	Eleven	Skipton
215	Burnley	Twenty two	Skipton, Barnoldswick with Settle one trip.
216	Skipton Horse Close Circular	Seven	Skipton
580	Giggleswick	Ten with another two to Settle	Skipton, Barnoldswick four Saturday only, and Settle (most).

Operated by a fleet of fourteen buses.

The NYCC had to step in to give some level of service and used minibuses during the daytime only, with no evening or weekend services. These were the twelve Carleton/fourteen Embsay/sixteen Skipton local.

NYCC initially also put on three services a day to Settle with three shorts to Hellifield. This soon stopped as from July 2014, on the A65 "main drag", things got better and a 580/581 Kirkby Lonsdale via Ingleton and Settle service was started in July 2014. This initially ran on Mon-Sat every 2 hours using two buses operated by Kirkby Lonsdale Coaches as the "Craven Connection" service. Ably supported by Colin Speakman of the Dales Bus organisation, further expansion came on 5th March 2018 when the service worked from Kirkby Lonsdale through to Lancaster (route 582). This also prevented KLC running empty to/from Kirkby Lonsdale from their newly-located depot at White Lund in Morecambe. So, a degree of normality returned to the A65 route care of KLC whose website is a joy to see, for example: https://klch.co.uk/calendar-gallery.

Pennine Fleet: In-service Post-War

Most of the fleet, the half cab post-war receipts and the Leyland Royal Tigers have already been illustrated in this book, or in the earlier *Skipton, 1967, with Pennine, Laycock, Ribble and West Yorkshire buses* published by Stenlake in 2020. Here we show those not already illustrated and also representations of the types of buses operated by Pennine.

JWT 724 Leyland PS/1 with Burlingham body was with Pennine from 1950 to 1963 and the last of three similar Leyland PS buses with Burlingham bodies that were very similar to Ribble's 201 to 247. New in May 1950 it was later converted to one-man operation but then failed a Ministry examination in December 1963 and was withdrawn and quickly replaced by ex Ribble all-Leyland PSU1/13 ECK 610. The engine though was salvaged, machined locally, and converted to horizontal for use in a Royal Tiger. JWT 724 is representative of three similar Leyland Tiger/Burlingham buses and with two coach bodied ones, were the "new" buys by Pennine from 1947 to 1950. From 1950 to 1954 came five Leyland Royal Tigers which included two former Leyland demonstrators. (Of interest in the background is an all-Leyland double decker of Burnley, Colne and Nelson that is working on the joint route with Ribble 281 to Colne via Earby. BCN operated to Skipton only on Saturdays and Summer Sundays). OS

Pennine bought a few Leyland demonstrators. MTC 757 was a 1950 PSU1/13 with Brush body that was at the 1950 Commercial Motor Show. It was with Pennine from 1951 to 1967 and ran up around 825,000 miles.

Entering the Gargrave depot and also at the 1950 Show was MTD 235, a Leyland PSU1/15 with the prototype Leyland coach body that was bought by many BET fleets, especially Ribble. It came to Pennine in 1952 and was withdrawn in 1971 and then stored for over 30 years by Pennine. After the closedown, it was retained by the Simpson family and was eventually sold in 2017 for preservation. Peter Gaunt, Ribble Enthusiasts Club

Three Leyland Royal Tigers came in 1953/1954. LWY 702 with a Leyland bus body and NWT 329/807 with Roe bus bodies. 702 and 329 are seen later, and 807 is above on layover at Skipton. Tony Greaves

A one off, VTD 214 was another ex-Leyland demonstrator of their Comet model with designation ECPO2/1R and had appeared at the 1954 Commercial Motor Show. It came in December 1955 and had a normal Duple Vega coach body and is seen above in Leeds bound for Blackpool on a Saturday hire to West Yorkshire. It was eventually said to be too small with just 36 seats and was sold on in 1961 to Bronte of Haworth.

Duple Donington's

The Donington was built between 1957 and 1962 and Pennine's first was a Leyland Tiger Cub, UWX 277 that was new in 1958 with bus seating. It worked until 1973 when it then saw further service with Browns of Guildford. The batch of four Donningtons replaced Tigers AWX 764, GWT 317/8 and HYG 60.

New in 1960 6108 WU was another seven bay Duple Donington with dual purpose seating. Awaiting "direction" in Skipton Bus Station, it was withdrawn in 1973 and went to Tillingbourne.

A five bay "cleaner"-looking 1961 Duple Donington 9712 WX was the last Tiger Cub they bodied. Parked near to the Jerry Croft, Skipton depot in the large car park, it would be withdrawn in 1972, the first Donington to go, and it also went to Tillingbourne.

Close to the Skipton Bus Station entrance, Leyland Leopard 5985 YG was the last Duple Donington to be bodied in 1962. Withdrawn in 1974 it saw further service with Beresford, where it served for many years as a crew "shed" at their depot. Like all the Doningtons, Pennine had replaced them with Plaxton Elite Express as, by this time, these were the standard buses. These Plaxtons were four from Laycock in 1972, followed by new ones from 1972 to 1982, then second-hand ones until 1994 when the Leyland Nationals "took over".

Leyland Leopards

240 CWY with Roe 8ft 2½in wide body was new in 1963. It went in 1975 and was another bus sold to Tillingbourne. (Similar bus LWU 499D is seen later). It is said Pennine would have preferred to buy Duple Doningtons but Duple withdrew the model in 1962. Tony Greaves

A 30-foot Leopard/Willowbrook 41-seater was bought in 1968 to replace MTC 757. Pennine was under the impression that 36 footers would not "fit" their routes but on finding this was not the case, UWU 521F (above, has a front window sticker for Butlins Camp) soon left in 1970.

In the autumn late day sun are CWU 101H and HWY 816J. They were two of four with BET style Willowbrook bodies from 1969 to 1971 with slight differences in the front time, front top vents, and front direction indicators. They replaced post-war Royal Tigers (MTC 235, LWT 702, ECK 610 and FWX 554C, the latter having replaced Tiger HYG 309 in 1965, all these buses are shown in my "Skipton, 1967" book). The four served until 1984/1985 before replacement by Plaxton Supreme Express second-hand buses. Tony Greaves

Plaxton Elite Express

OWR 265 (and 266) K were the first new bus grant Elite Express buses bought by Pennine in 1972. This would be on a run via Carleton to Barnoldswick. The other Elites were MYG 759 to 761K, OWY 197K ex-Laycock and those bought new were UWU 596L, RWY 378/379M, JWU 797 to 799N, (OWR 197K and JWU 798N are also shown in "Skipton, 1967" book). The lightweight ex-Laycock Bedford MYGs went in 1975, and the Leopards left between 1991 and 1994.

JWU 797N on the 09.27 Morecambe – Skipton, has just left Lancaster Bus Station on 23rd August 1975. R. Downham

RHE 30M, with 31M and 32M, were new to Yorkshire Traction in 1974 and came to Pennine in 1986 to booster the fleet for the new Burnley route. Two lasted until 1989 and 31M went in 1991.

Plaxton Supreme Express

Seven of these were re-registered in 1994/95 with JIL registrations. Five of these registrations were later used on Leyland Nationals. Then three of these registrations were to be used again, on later Leyland Nationals! Confusing? Certainly!

UWR 712R was the first Plaxton Supreme Express in 1977. The Supreme was externally different from the Elite with its stepped trimming above the front wheel. This bus was later re-registered as JIL 7417 and withdrawn in 1995 as YUG 71R. The JIL 7417 registration was also used on LN8 from 1995, then next on LN15 from 1999. UWR 712R was followed in 1978 by AUA 965S (later JIL 7416) which went in 1996.

The last new Supreme was NWT 839V that came in 1980 and in 1994 became JIL 4698. It shows the Express body version. It was withdrawn in 1997 when the JIL registration went to LN11.

JIL 2426 was originally BTL 485X and new in 1981 to Marfleet Coaches in Binbrook, Lincolnshire who closed in 1982. It came to Pennine in 1984 from Wing of Sleaford, Lincolnshire and was the last Supreme to be withdrawn in 2009. It had a different livery, using cream instead of grey as it mainly did private hire work. It was the first of many second-hand Supremes bought up to 1990, e.g. TPL 762X, NPA 220W (JIL 2428), YGE 635S, SOA 681S, UDW 140S, OCK 452T (shown next), with the last Plaxton being OUF 50W (MAP 347W and JIL 2427).

New to Fishwick, Leyland in 1979 as OCK 452T, it came to Pennine in 1989 and is seen here in the Gargrave premises. Re-registered JIL 4653 in 1994 after withdrawal in 1995 it was converted to a tow truck and registered HWR 449T. The JIL number plate then passed to LN9 in 1996 and next to LN16 in 2001.

Leyland Nationals

The Leyland National was a joint venture between British Leyland and the National Bus Company who bought many of the over 7,000 built between 1972 and 1985. It was built integrally, the steel body having no separate chassis and was in two lengths for the UK market, of 10.3 metres (33'9") and 11.3 metres (37'), and with a choice of single or dual doors. The engines were mainly Leyland with the Mark 2 version from 1979 offering an optional Gardner engine.

The first ones came to Pennine in 1994 and overall, nineteen short ones were used in service numbered LN1 to 12, 14 to 20; three others were bought for spares. They came from many companies and had been new between 1975 and 1978 with two from 1980 (LN6) and 1981 (LN11). Bought originally by larger companies like London Transport, London Country, Crosville, and Alexander Midland, they came to Pennine between 1994 and 2001 mainly from the second owners. They all received JIL registrations apart from LN2 that came with RIB 5081.

Most of them served Pennine for ten years, with the last ones leaving in 2009. Whatever one's opinion is of Leyland Nationals, with Pennine they had long service lives and from new, a life of between 21 and 30 years.

LN4 outbound leaving Gargrave new in 1977 to London Transport as OJD 879R, then London Busways and with Pennine from 1994 to 2004. Phil Howard

LN6 and 11 were later model National 2 models, with a front grill. They came respectively in 1995 and 1997 from West Yorkshire (PWY 583W new in 1980) and Ribble (JCK 847W new in 1981) As was normal in the later days of Pennine, some minor livery variations were not unusual. Both went in 2004 and were replaced

Dennis Darts

The bus of choice from 2003, 29 came before 2014. Numbered with a D prefix from 1 to 12, 14 to 19, and to complicate matters fleet numbers D1, 2, 4 to 8, 11, were used twice, D3 was used three times and one Dart did not get a number!

Dennis of Guildford had launched their lightweight rear-engined Dennis Dart in 1988 as a midibus that had a rear engine and high floor and Plaxton also launched their Pointer body. The model evolved as MPD (midibus pointer dart) and offered varied lengths from 8.5 to 9.8 metres, with the longer SPD (super pointer dart) up to 11.3 metres. In 1995 came the low floor model and this was designated as the SLF (super low floor).

Mainly bodied by Plaxton as the Pointer, others also bodied the Dart, including Northern Counties of Wigan (who were to be bought by Plaxton in 1995) and Wright from Northern Ireland.

In 1998, the owner of Alexander Coachbuilders took over Dennis and soon, also Plaxton. Then in 2004, Plaxton and Alexander Dennis were sold to separate companies. As the Pointer was already by now being built by Alexander, it became an Alexander Dennis product and Plaxton went on to do different things. In 2006 the Alexander Dennis Enviro200 Dart replaced the Pointer Dart.

Pennine had nineteen Darts in service at the end in 2014. A selection of their Dart fleet follows.

Three Dart MPDs with body builder variants wait in Skipton. Left to right, these are Wright, Plaxton and Northern Counties. In total Pennine had six Wrights, seventeen Plaxtons, one Northern Counties and five Alexanders.

Working back from Burnley, D1 with Wright body came to Pennine in 2003 and was the first of six Darts in that year. New in 1992 to Tynemouth & District, it was withdrawn in 2011.

D2 with Wright body in Skipton Bus Station. Also, one new to Tynemouth & District, it was the first one withdrawn by Pennine in 2007.

D10 came in 2006 from Metrobus and was an "original" high floor Plaxton MPD was new in 1995. It left Pennine in 2012.

D1 (2012 issue) came to Pennine in 2012 and is inbound and just past Coniston Cold on the A65 and soon will go under the railway bridge that carries the line from Skipton to Settle for either Carlisle or Carnforth. Don McKeown

Leaving Skipton, D3 (second issue) came to Pennine in 2006 and had an Alexander Dash style body. It was new in 1996 to Midland Red Rugby and withdrawn by Pennine in 2014.

Alexander/Dart D6 (second issue) at Malham. This was a later SLF version that was new in 2002 to Clynog & Trevor in Wales. Don McKeown

The Fleet on the Routes

Pennine operated in the beautiful countryside that is part of the Yorkshire Dales National Park. This section will look at Pennine at work, principally in their final years.

AWX 763 heads back from Skipton to Gargrave with a good load. The chassis finished up being used in Malta.

Malham

240 CWY outbound in Skipton High Street for Malham. PM Photography

Outbound UDW 140S on Skipton High Street.

CWT 474H nearing Skipton Bus Station on 13th July 1978. R Downham

GWT 317 is in the bus station with a wrong blind spelling and whilst recognised as a mistake – it however, carried on for some years!

HYG 309, a Leyland PS2 with Burlingham body from 1949. Plaxton Panorama-bodied FWX 554C replaced it in 1965. PM Photography

HWU 816J leaving Skipton for Malham on 5th August 1979. R Downham

CWT 474H leaves Skipton by Skipton Girls High School on Gargrave Road and is heading for the A65. PM

D5 (second issue) to Pennine in 2012, on the A65 approaching Gargrave for Malham. Don McKeown

D5 crosses the River Aire near Airton heading for Malham. Don McKeown

1997 Plaxton/Dart D15 came in 2008 heading for Malham. New to East London Bus & Coach, as was D2 (second issue) and D14. This bus is now in preservation and was the last to leave Pennine in 2015. Don McKeown

Plaxton/Dart D15 continues its journey to Malham. Don McKeown

Plaxton/Dart D15 waits its departure time in Malham. It had over 20 enthusiasts on board, ten school children and three others. It was the last Malham to Skipton journey. Don McKeown

Leyland/Roe 1953 NWT 329 in 1971 returns from Malham with Malham Cove visible near the mid horizon. The Cove is a mile from the village and in the hills above is Malham Tarn. This is the source of the River Aire and flows underground to appear at the foot of the Cove, continuing for over 90 miles passing Skipton, Keighley, Bingley, Saltaire, Leeds, Castleford, and Knottingley. The River Aire empties into the River Ouse at Airmyn, ("myn" being an old English word for river mouth). Eventually the River Ouse flows into the Humber and the North Sea. Keith Newton

OWR 266M Plaxton Elite Express, new to Pennine in 1972, leaves Malham behind in August 1980. It was withdrawn in 1991 with sister bus 265K. Keith Newton

NWT 329 on 20th April 1973 with Malham in the background. Long serving with Pennine from 1953 to 1974 with its sister (NWT 807), they were replaced by new Plaxton Elites RWY 378/9M. Keith

Plaxton/Dart D15 returning from Malham heading for Gargrave and Skipton. Don McKeown

NWT 329 crosses the River Aire returning from Malham. Keith Newton

Leyland/Willowbrook CWU 101H new in 1970 working back from Malham. With three other similar buses, they formed the backbone of the stage fleet from 1971 to 1984. It was replaced in 1984 by a second-hand Plaxton Supreme. Keith Newton

LN5 near to Gargrave, came to Pennine in 1994 having been new in 1973 to Southern Vectis. Withdrawn in 2005 and replaced by a Dart. Keith Newton

CWU 101H heads for Gargrave and Skipton. Keith Newton

Carleton

Plaxton/Dart D7 (second issue) in Skipton from Carleton. It was the last Dart bought in 2014 and had been new in 2001 to Central Parking of London Heathrow. Don McKeown

Plaxton (Alexander in some listings)/Dart D3 (second issue) heads out to Carleton. New in 2002 to Thames Travel and the next to the last Dart in 2014. Don McKeown

Outbound D7 (2014 second issue) is on the River Aire bridge heading for Carleton. Don McKeown

1995 Dart/Plaxton D10 from Carleton heads across the flood plain towards the River Aire. New to Hylton Castle, it came to Pennine in 2006 and left in 2012. Don McKeown

D10 approaches Carleton. Don McKeown

Carleton and the Dart has just left the bus stop on the left with a right turn back to Skipton. Don McKeown

Plaxton Dart D19 leaves Carleton behind. New in 2000 to Bus Eireann in Dublin it was one of three (D17 to 19) that came to Pennine in 2010. Don McKeown

Embsay

RWY 379M was a Leyland Leopard with Plaxton Elite Express body, new in 1974 along with RWY 378M. The latter went in October 1980 after a fire, but 379M stayed until 1993 to be replaced by a Leyland National.

LN19 approaches the Castle roundabout at the top of Skipton High Street bound for Embsay.
Don McKeown

D4 (second issue in 2012) arrives at Skipton by the Castle roundabout. With an Alexander body it was new in 2002 to Simmonds of Botesdale. Don McKeown

D12 leaves the Castle roundabout and heads up the hill for Embsay. New in 1996 to Thames Transit it came to Pennine in 2008. Don McKeown

D2 (second issue in 2007) has just run under the railway bridge for the Skipton/Rylstone freight only branch line to the Swinden Limeworks. D2 was new in 1997 to East London, as were D14/15. Don McKeown

D7 (second issue in 2014) heads back to Skipton with the bypass road bridge behind. Don McKeown

D7 (second issue 2014) on Skipton Road for East Lane to Embsay (the vacant land of the left is now all housing). Don McKeown

D7 (second issue in 2014) leaves East Lane and enters Shires Lane in Embsay at the start of the turning loop in the village. This went via Shires Lane and Low Lane for Main Street. Don McKeown

D15 at Embassy on the last departure from Embsay Main Street. Don McKeown

LN5 leaves Embsay Main Street and heads back towards East Lane for, despite the blind, Skipton. Originally XDL 800L with Southern Vectis in 1973, it came to Pennine in 1994 and stayed until 2005. Keith Newton

Burnley and Barnoldswick

RHE 32M lays over in Skipton. One of three Leyland Leopards (RHE 30 to 32M) with Plaxton Elite Express bodies new to Yorkshire Traction in 1974 it came to Pennine in 1984. Reportedly bought to booster the fleet on the Burnley run, they stayed until 1989/90 when they were replaced by newer Plaxton Supreme Express Leopards.

LN4 was originally operated by London Country as SPC 279R and has run in from Burnley. It was new in 1977 and served Pennine between 1994 and 2004.

D6 (second issue 2012) entering Skipton will soon pass the railway station. Don McKeown

D18 heads out of Skipton near the railway station. One of three (D17 to 19) new in 2000 to Bus Eireann and with Pennine from 2010.

D1 (second issue 2012) on Broughton Road leaving Skipton and passing Niffany Corner near where the former Skipton to Colne railway left the main line. The barrier on the left protects the towpath on the Leeds and Liverpool Canal. D1 had been new in 2002 to an operator in West Bromwich. Don McKeown

June 1979 and RWY 378M leaves West Marton on Gledstone Road having left the A59 from Skipton on the former Laycock route to Barnoldswick. Pennine eventually abandoned this A59 East & West Marton leg to run via Thornton-in-Craven and left East & West Marton to the tendered Skipton to Preston route. The Leopard/Plaxton Elite Express was new in 1974 and left in October 1980 after it caught fire and burnt out. Keith Newton

D18 inbound approaching Thornton-in-Craven. Don McKeown

D6 (2012 second issue) outbound at Thornton-in-Craven. Don McKeown

D1 (2012 second issue) approaches Kelbrook for Barnoldswick. It came from Home James Travel, Speke in 2012. Don McKeown

D6 (2012 second issue) from Skipton at the Kelbrook roundabout for Burnley. Don McKeown

D5 (2012 second issue) leaves the Kelbrook roundabout for Barnoldswick and Skipton. Don McKeown

D8 at Main Street, Colne on one of the Burnley to Barnoldswick "short" journeys. New in 1995 to Yorkshire Blue Bus it ran with Pennine from 2004 to 2012. Don McKeown

D19 at the now one-way Station Road at Barnoldswick and heading for Burnley. The twelve letters of Barnoldswick were used on the clock face. Don McKeown

RHE 31W is further up Station Road at the Barnoldswick Conservative Club (and when this road was two way). Keith Newton

D4 (second issue 2012) in Barnoldswick on the later, once a day journey on route 211. Don McKeown

D11 (second issue 2013) approaches Colne from Barnoldswick and passes the Upper Foulridge Reservoir. Don McKeown

D18 leaves Burnley Bus Station. Don McKeown

D8 (second issue 2012) waits departure at Burnley on the last ever journey. Don McKeown

Skipton Locals

H313/314 WUA were unusual Leyland Swifts with Reeves Burgess DP39F bodies new in April 1991 and quickly sold in January 1992 to Stevensons of Uttoxeter. This early sale was reported as due to poor quality, brakes and after sales service. Ominously, they were the last new buses purchased by Pennine.

D6 (second issue 2012) at Caroline Square in Skipton enters Newmarket Street on a clockwise journey of the local route. It will soon pass the former West Yorkshire bus depot. Don McKeown

D11 (second issue 2012) at the top of Shortbank Road and will eventually head towards Greatwood Avenue for North Parade. Don McKeown

D6 (second issue 2012) running clockwise from Shortbank Road and on Moorview Way heading for Hurrs Road. Don McKeown

Settle, Ingleton, Lancaster, Morecambe

1954 Royal Tiger/Roe NWT 807 is bound for Ingleton with a Ribble on the X43 to Manchester. PM

1965 FWX 554C on a short to Settle was the first of many Plaxtons bought by Pennine and was in the cream and orange coach livery when new.

1971 HWU 816J Leopard/Willowbrook BET lookalike, lays over. The positioning of the side fleet name style may be noted. *PM*

Bedford/Plaxton Elite Express MYG 759K was new to Laycock in 1972 (with MWR 760/761K). It has just left Skipton Bus Station where the West Yorkshire Bristol RE behind is leaving. The three lightweight Bedfords soon left Pennine in 1975. *PM*

AUA 965S approaches Caroline Square, Skipton with behind, Burton the tailors shop. This was the penultimate new bus and was a Leyland Leopard with Plaxton Supreme Express body new in 1978 which became JIL 7416 in 1995 and was withdrawn in 1996. This JIL plate went to LN9 and then to LN18 in 2001. PM

Inbound 1966 Leyland Leopard/Roe LWU 499D turns from the High Street in Skipton at Caroline Square. It left Pennine in 1975 and was replaced by a new JWU registered Leopard/Plaxton Elite Express. PM

D15 arrives in Skipton from Mill Bridge on the last day and will run down the High Street towards Caroline Square. Don McKeown

LN3 inbound at Gargrave. Phil Howard

Outbound OWR 265K pauses in Gargrave.

HWU 817J heads down the A65 towards Gargrave. PM

D1 (2012 second issue) inbound on the bridge over the River Aire past Coniston Cold. Don McKeown

Outbound JWU 799N at Hellifield on 1135hours from Skipton to Ingleton on Saturday 4th April 1981. R. Downham

D4 (2012 second issue) passes through Long Preston.

KL52 LZX leaves Settle. Never numbered, it came in 2013 with D11 from Sovereign Bus & Coach and had this different livery. Don McKeown

D8 (2012 second issue) kneel loading at Settle. Don McKeown

Outbound OWR 266K loads in Settle on market day bound for Ingleton. New in 1972 it stayed with Pennine until 1991.

Inbound OWR 265K at Settle on the 1250 hours from Lancaster on 4th April 1981. R. Downham

LWY 702 lays over at Settle.

One of the two NWTs lays over in the car park at Settle, in front of a well-sheeted flatbed truck.

On 4th April 1981, JWU 797N has returned to Settle with the 1335 hours from Skipton and parked up awaiting to work the 1534 hours back to Skipton. R. Downham

Outbound D1 (2012 second issue) leaves Settle behind and has come over the River Ribble bridge and is now on a short run to Giggleswick with the return blind already set. Don McKeown

D8 and the first Plaxton Dart in 2004, enters Giggleswick to turn round. Don McKeown

D5 was one of three Wright/Darts (D4 to D6) new to Tynemouth & District in 1993, on the short downhill from the main road for the turn at Giggleswick. It was withdrawn in 2012. Don McKeown

The last passenger leaves D11 (2013 second issue) at the bottom of the hill. The bus now swings right before reversing back to load. Don McKeown

D1 (second issue in 2012) loads at Giggleswick. Don McKeown

D7 Dart/Northern Counties pulls away from Giggleswick terminus. New in 1995 to Speedlink London Heathrow it served Pennine from 2004 to 2013. Don McKeown

D4 climbs the hill to join, at the top, the old A65 road to Settle for Skipton. Don McKeown

CWT 474H in 1979 outbound from Settle at Rathmell and heading for Tosside. Keith Newton

LWU 499D ascends Buckhaw Brow on 16th May 1971 with Settle in the mid right background. It is on the then main A65 road; the A65 later used the newly built 4-mile bypass opened in December 1988 that ran from before Settle to near to the top of Buckhaw Brow. The Pennine buses, however, still ran via Settle. Keith Newton

RWY 379W ascends Buckhaw Brow in June 1979 outbound for Ingleton. Keith Newton

AWX 763 crests Buckhaw Brow heading for Ingleton. It was reported in the Craven Herald *15 Oct 2011, "At a time when Pennine buses laboured up Buckhaw Brow on their way from Settle to Ingleton, it was such a popular run on a sunny Sunday that a Mr Robinson erected a stall by the head of the Brow and sold fruit, vegetables and rabbits".*

Clapham with OWR 266K inbound and another story from the Craven Herald*: "There was a day when, as I was travelling from Clapham to Skipton, a goat was among the passengers. I also heard the story – which may or may not be true – of an old lady who boarded the bus creakily, bought a ticket for Skipton and asked the man at the wheel to drive carefully. She was going to the hospital. As she left the bus in town, the driver asked her how she felt. "I'm alright," was the reply. "I've got a jelly in this bag – and it hadn't quite set when I left home.""*

CWU 101H loads at Ingleton for Lancaster. OS

NWT 329 waits off stand in Lancaster with a Ribble all-Leyland coach at the side and possibly two SMT AEC Monocoaches at the back. OS

At Lancaster is the first Donnington UWX 277.

6108 WU on stand in Lancaster. Peter Gaunt REC

9712 WX leaves Lancaster Bus Station for Skipton.

Resting off stand at Lancaster Bus Station, with the driver reading his newspaper on the 40-minute layover. In the early 1950s this was a 3-hour 10-minute journey from Skipton but reduced in the 1960s to 2 hours 24 minutes. FWX 554C from 1965 was the first of many Plaxtons bought by Pennine and was in the cream and orange coach livery when new. It had replaced Leyland PS HYG 309 in 1965 but only stayed until 1971 when it was replaced by a Leyland/Willowbrook HWU 816J. Perhaps its manual front door could have been a problem on stage work, as Pennine was all OPO by 1970. PM Photography

Inbound from Morecambe in Lancaster OWR 266K and has just left Lancaster Bus Station, on 31st May 1975 bound for Skipton. In 1986 this duty started from Ingleton at 07.32 and arrived at Morecambe 08.59, then left for Skipton on the 09.31 Morecambe to Skipton due at 12.11. Leaving Skipton on route 581 at 12.43, arriving back at Lancaster at 15.10, from where it returned to Skipton at 15.50 on a 581 arriving at 18.11. Leaving Skipton on a 581 at 18.43 and in Lancaster at 21.10, it then finally, left on the 580 at 21.50, arriving back in Ingleton at 22.47. R Downham

A rare picture of Pennine in Morecambe – however RWY 378M is on an excursion. Behind in Lancaster blue is a former Morecambe Leyland/Massey in the fleet number series 87 to 89. The Morecambe CT fleet combined with Lancaster CT in 1974. OS

The ex-Laycock OWY 197K is on a scheduled layover between 0859 and 0931 at Euston Road Bus Station, Morecambe on 22nd April 1986 on the daily single Lancaster to Skipton trip. This was soon to finish, in October 1986.

References

Donald Binns (2000), *Pennine Motor Services, 1925 to 2000*

Neville Mercer (2015), *Independent Bus Operators in Western Yorkshire.*

The P.S.V. Circle (October 1969), *Fleet History PB5, The Small Stage Carriage Operators of the Yorkshire Traffic Area (Part1).*

Stuart Emmett (Stenlake Publishing Ltd, 2020), *Skipton, 1967 with Pennine, Laycock, Ribble and West Yorkshire Buses.*

Stuart Emmett (Key Publishing, 2021), *Yorkshire Dales Buses, West Yorkshire Road Car Company in Wharfedale, The 1950s to the 1970s.*

The Local Transport History Library (2020), *Pennine Motor Services 1925 to 2014*

Omnibus Society, *NW & Yorkshire Monthly Bulletins*, varied dates

West Yorkshire Information Service, newssheets, varied dates